7 Devotional Disciplines
Copyright © 1993
Revised 2018
ISBN 13 is 9781979048521
ISBN 10 1979048525
All rights reserved.

Scripture taken from the New King James Version®.
Copyright © 1982 by Thomas Nelson.
Used by permission. All rights reserved.

Thanks to
Sandy Muller,
Rebecca Soule,
and Faith Muller
for their invaluable support,
and to
Daniela Petkova,
Bill Powell,
Craig Cunningham, and
Reilly Dussia
for editing this book.

Contents

Introduction 1
1. Prayer: The Discipline of Intimacy 4
2. Fasting: The Discipline of Privation . . . 18
3. Bible Reading: The Discipline of Study . 27
4. Praise: The Discipline of Adoration . . . 38
5. Witness: The Discipline of Compassion . 43
6. Giving: The Discipline of Dependence. . 54
7. Fellowship: The Discipline of Friendship
   and Unity 60

Introduction

"The time is fulfilled, and the kingdom of God is at hand. Repent, and believe in the gospel!" That is the message Jesus proclaimed (Mark 1:15). "Gospel" means "good news." It is certainly good news that "God loved the world so much that He gave His only Son, that whoever believes in Him should not perish but have eternal life" (John 3:16). Without the Lord Jesus Christ, each of us is a sinner each of us is lost. "For all have sinned and fall short of the glory of God" (Romans 3:23). In contrast, God is holy, and He is a righteous Judge. The righteous judgment of God that our sin deserves is eternal punishment. In the most glorious, noble, and gracious act ever done, God's Son, Jesus Christ, paid for our sins by dying for us on the cross. He took upon Himself our sin and suffered the penalty for our sin. That satisfied the righteous requirement of God. When Jesus rose from the dead, we who believe in Him were born again to a living hope.

God is a King, and when we accept His authority in our lives by turning from our sin and believing in Jesus Christ, our eternal life begins! Eternal life is much more than just "existing"; like our earthly life, growth is to characterize our eternal life. Also like earthly life, although spiritual growth (also called growing or maturing in Christ) happens naturally, it requires attention and nourishment . Scripture commands to "be even more diligent to make your call and election sure" (2 Peter 1:10), and to "work out your own salvation with fear and trembling" (Philippians 2:12). There are things we can do to facilitate our spiritual growth, but ultimately it is "God who gives the increase" (1 Corinthians 3:7).

This book provides believers in the Lord Jesus Christ with guidelines to practice seven disciplines essential for spiritual growth: prayer, fasting, Bible study, praise, witnessing, giving, and fellowship with other believers. Although each of them is mentioned, commended, and commanded in the Bible, nowhere does the Bible itself list all seven together. In the following pages, these seven disciplines are presented in a concise, practical guide to help people get started, not as an exhaustive or comprehensive text. That is, this practical

Introduction

guide provides principles and suggestions for Christian believers who have a sincere desire to grow in Christ. These principles are to be applied under the leading of the Holy Spirit, grounded in Holy Scriptures, and with the liberty of the Holy Spirit to modify them according to the individual needs of the believer.

Scripture references are given (usually in parentheses) in the following format:

book chapter:verse. Additional chapters are separated by semicolons (;). Examples:

John 3:16 = The Gospel of John, chapter 3, verse 16.

1 John 2:15 = The first epistle of John, chapter 2, verse 15.

Jude 6 = The letter of Jude (which has only 1 chapter) verse 6.

John 17 = The Gospel of John, chapter 17, entire chapter.

John 3:16-18 = The Gospel of John, chapter 3, verses 16, 17, 18.

John 3:16,21 = The Gospel of John, chapter 3, verses 16 and 21.

Job 1:12; 2:5 = Job chapter 1 verse 12, and chapter 2 verse 5.

The devotional disciplines discussed here—and all spiritual endeavors—must be practiced in relation to the gospel of the kingdom of God. In other words, they must be based on the foundation of the Lordship of Christ in our lives and must be centered around Jesus Christ Himself. The Ten Commandments begin, "Hear, O Israel: The LORD our God, the LORD is one!" (Deuteronomy 6:4). In other words, we are to pay attention to what God tells us. All the prayer, fasting, Bible study, and church attendance we do will not make us grow spiritually if our hearts ultimately turn away from the Lord Himself. Instead, our hearts must be like the heart of ancient King David, who wrote in Psalm 27:8, "When You said, 'Seek My face,' My heart said to You, 'Your face, LORD, I will seek.'" As you seek the Lord's face, recall what Jesus' mother told the servants at the wedding feast: "Whatever He says to you, do it!" In order to

Introduction

benefit from the seven devotional disciplines (or any devotional), we must obey what God tells us – always, promptly, and completely.

May the Lord be with you and bless you as you read and seek to apply these principles in your life! Walking with Jesus Christ is a beautiful and incredible thing. The more we know Him, the more wonderful we see that He is!

1. Prayer
The Discipline of Intimacy

In response to the disciples' question, "Lord, teach us to pray" (Luke 11:1), the Lord Jesus gave them a model prayer, found in Matthew 6:9-13 & Luke 11:2-4.

The Model Prayer of Matthew 6

"Our Father in heaven" (Matthew 6:9)
How we are to address God the Father.

We are to pray by the Holy Spirit, through Jesus Christ the Son, to the Father. "For there is one God and one Mediator between God and men, the Man Christ Jesus," (1 Timothy 2:5). This means that we are not to pray to or through any other individuals as we address God the Father. This includes the figures of Mary, the saints, our ancestors, or even the dead. The prophet Isaiah warns against this when he writes, "And when they say to you, 'Seek those who are mediums and wizards, who whisper and mutter,' should not a people seek their God? Should they seek the dead on behalf of the living?" (Isaiah 8:19).. Instead, Jesus gave Himself for us, to bring us to God: "For Christ also suffered once for sins, the just for the unjust, that He might bring us to God, being put to death in the flesh but made alive by the Spirit," (1 Peter 3:18). As a result, we have a relationship with God as our true Father, and we are to relate to Him as our Father. (See John 6:32-65 for Jesus' own relationship with the Father.) How are we to pray? By simply talking to God – not in special tones of voice, or with a contrived religious attitude. What makes it prayer? Simply talking to God—not special tones of voice, or a contrived religious attitude. Nor should we only pray in certain postures. For example, there are at least 10 types of postures mentioned in the Bible in which people prayed:

The Discipline of Intimacy

1. With bowed head (Exodus 34:8-9)
2. Bowed down with face between the knees (1 Kings 18:42)
3. Standing (1 Kings 19:11,13,14)
4. Sitting (1 Chronicles 17:16)
5. On the knees with hands spread to the Lord (Ezra 9:5)
6. On a bed (Psalm 4:4; 6:6, 2 Kings 20:1-2)
7. With face on the ground (Matthew 26:39—Jesus' first prayer in the Garden of Gethsemane)
8. Kneeling (Luke 22:41—Jesus' second or third prayer in the Garden)
9. With feet in stocks (Acts 16:24-25)
10. Lifting up hands (1 Timothy 2:8).

We may pray in any posture!

Neither are we to pray only in certain places or at certain times., Several places are mentioned in the New Testament alone: an inner room (Matthew 6:6), the wilderness (Luke 5:16), an upper room (Acts 1:13-14), the temple (Acts 3:1), a housetop (Acts 10:9), in jail (Acts 16:24-25). In fact, the Bible specifically teaches that we are to pray everywhere: "I desire therefore that the men pray everywhere, lifting up holy hands, without wrath and doubting," (1 Timothy 2:8). Furthermore, the Bible tells us that there are not only certain times of prayer, but that we are to pray at all times (Ephesians 6:18) and without ceasing (1 Thessalonians 5:17). We are to be "vigilant" in prayer (Colossians 4:2).

Finally, the Bible does not teach that we are to only use certain words, or only special words. We can pray with our understanding (in a language that we know) or we can pray in "tongues" (in an earthly or heavenly language that we do not know). In fact, we are to do both (1 Corinthians 14:15). When we pray in tongues, we edify ourselves (1 Corinthians 14:4) and build up our faith (Jude 20), and when we pray in our native language we edify those who hear us.

Even so you, since you are zealous for spiritual gifts, let it be for

Chapter 1: Prayer

the edification of the church that you seek to excel. Therefore let him who speaks in a tongue pray that he may interpret. For if I pray in a tongue, my spirit prays, but my understanding is unfruitful. What is the conclusion then? I will pray with the spirit, and I will also pray with the understanding. I will sing with the spirit, and I will also sing with the understanding.
(1 Corinthians 14:12-15).

Almost all of us feel something is "not right" deep inside of us from time to time, without apparent reason. Our spirit within us may be perceiving an evil spirit around us or the Holy Spirit may be laying a burden on our heart for the purpose of prayer. When we have knowledge of the specific situation, individual, etc., we can pray with our understanding. Otherwise, we can pray in tongues. "Likewise the Spirit also helps in our weaknesses. For we do not know what we should pray for as we ought, but the Spirit Himself makes intercession for us with groanings which cannot be uttered," (Romans 8:26). The apostles themselves learned to be alert to such things. They knew what seemed good to the Holy Spirit: "For it seemed good to the Holy Spirit, and to us, to lay upon you no greater burden than these necessary things," (Acts 15:28).

A man of God once related the following account. There was a missionary who came to a remote tribe to preach the gospel. He was taken to a hut where a naked, lunatic, demonized woman (in other words, a woman under the influence of demons or "demon possessed") was kept in a cage. He commanded the demons to depart from her, and began to feel intense oppression, to the point that he collapsed in exhaustion. He prayed, "Lord, have brother Robert pray!" At that time Robert, in Texas, awoke from sleep with a burden for the missionary. He began to pray in tongues, and wrote down the date, time, and burden that he felt. On a different continent, that missionary felt new strength, got up, and successfully cast the demons out of the woman. When the villagers saw the power of God, they turned to the Lord. Robert later asked the missionary what was happening at the date and time he noted, and it was confirmed that the time coincided with that of the incident.

"Hallowed be Your name" (Matthew 6:9)

Our primary motivation should be the Lord's glory.

As believers, it should be our desire to see Jesus revered and honored. The Bible states, "But You are holy, enthroned in the praises of Israel" (Psalm 22:3), and instructs us to do everything for the glory of God (1 Corinthians 10:31). We can begin our prayer time with thanksgiving, praise, and worship. The psalmist tells us to "Enter into His gates with thanksgiving, and into His courts with praise," (Psalm 100:4). Praying in this mindset will help us to see things from God's perspective and build our faith, as it reminds us of God's greatness and of previous answers to prayer. As we express our gratefulness to God through praise, it invites the Lord's presence into our prayer time.

Beginning our prayer time with thanksgiving and praise has a great "side effect": When we come into God's presence, we are convicted of sins we have committed., So if we come first with a heart of praise, it helps us to confess, repent, and ultimately be forgiven and receive answers to our prayers.

"Your kingdom come. Your will be done on earth as it is in heaven" (Matthew 6:10)

The purpose of prayer: So that God's kingdom and His will are expressed on earth as in heaven.

The kingdom of God refers to the reign (or "rule") of God. His kingdom exists wherever He is in authority. God rules on His throne in heaven; on earth, His rule extends to wherever His authority is acknowledged and obeyed. We are subjects of God's kingdom. Although our bodies exist in this present evil age (Galatians 1:4), spiritually we are seated in heavenly places in Christ Jesus (Ephesians 2:6). In that sense, we are actually living in God's kingdom now. From Christ's directive to pray "on earth as it is in heaven, " it seems that God wants earth to be like heaven.

Since, according to Matthew 6:10, we are to pray that His will be done on earth, we can conclude that He wants us to know His will. This should give us confidence when we pray, as the New

Testament book of First John clearly tells us: "Now this is the confidence that we have in Him, that if we ask anything according to His will, He hears us. And if we know that He hears us, whatever we ask, we know that we have the petitions that we have asked of Him," (1 John 5:14-15).

God's heart (His will) is to bless the nations by turning them from iniquities (Acts 3:26) to salvation in Jesus Christ (Acts 4:12). He has chosen us, His "house" (Hebrews 3:6), to pray for the nations (Isaiah 56:7). Coming to God on behalf of another person, group, or nation, is called intercession. Praying on their behalf is called intercessory prayer. God judges sin, but He looks for a man (Isaiah 41:28; 59:16) who will stand before God on behalf of another person, group, or nation. "So I sought for a man among them who would make a wall, and stand in the gap before Me on behalf of the land, that I should not destroy it; but I found no one" (Ezekiel 22:30). We can make a difference in history!

As part of praying for God's authority on earth, we are to also pray for the authorities that already exist on earth. We are specifically instructed to pray for those in authority: "Therefore I exhort first of all that supplications, prayers, intercessions, and giving of thanks be made for all men, for kings and all who are in authority, that we may lead a quiet and peaceable life in all godliness and reverence" (1 Timothy 2:1-2).

There are times when a gap will occur in the spiritual protection of a people or a nation (Ezekiel 13:5). As a result of this gap, which is a breach or open place in the spiritual protection because of sin, God is looking for people to stand before Him so that His wrath is turned away (Jeremiah 18:20). To do this, we need to know the Lord and have love for people, even to the point of weeping for them before God (Jeremiah 9:1). Jesus told us to pray that laborers be sent into the harvest (Matthew 9:37-38). In Christ, we can even have the nations as our inheritance—if we ask: "Ask of Me, and I will give You The nations for Your inheritance, And the ends of the earth for Your possession," (Psalm 2:8).

If we are praying according to God's will, we can pray in His name. "And whatever you ask in My name, that I will do, that the Father may be glorified in the Son. If you ask anything in My name, I will do it," (John 14:13-14). Praying "in Jesus' name" does not mean we simply put those words at the end of a prayer. It means to pray as Jesus' ambassadors according to His will (2 Corinthians 5:20). An ambassador can only make treaties as he has authorization by his government. For example, Jesus said, "If you remain in me and my words remain in you, ask whatever you wish, and it will be given you," (John 15:7). I know a young Bulgarian musician who felt the Lord put on his heart that he would have a music ministry and lead others in praise and worship. He needed a guitar **in order to fulfill the word of the Lord**, so he began to pray for a guitar. He asked very specifically for an expensive guitar, an Ovation, although the cost of a new Ovation would have been more than an annual Bulgarian salary at that time. A friend of his was visiting America, and someone gave him an Ovation guitar, which he then gave to the young musician when he returned to Bulgaria! This man did not arbitrarily pick something he wanted and then begin to pray for it. God had spoken something to his heart, and he believed it and acted upon it. God's word to him was his authorization to ask for something very specific. God then gave him whatever he asked, even though it may have seemed extravagant.

"Give us this day our daily bread" (Matthew 6:11)
This is called petition—asking God to meet our needs.

It is "OK" (and good!) to pray for our own needs. We should be specific when we pray, because specific prayers get specific answers. Although Jesus knew the needs of the people, He still asked them to clearly state what it was they wanted Him to do. "And answering him, Jesus said, 'What do you want Me to do for you?' And the blind man said to Him, 'Rabboni, I want to regain my sight!'" (Mark 10:51, NAS). Jesus Himself saw that the man was blind, but He wanted the man to say exactly what it was that he wanted. The disciples prayed for boldness (Acts 4:29), and they received the answer (Acts 4:31).

When we pray, we are to pray in faith (Matthew 21:22), not

with meaningless repetition. "And when you pray, do not use vain repetitions as the heathen do. For they think that they will be heard for their many words," (Matthew 6:7). Praying "Our Father who is in heaven ..." several times every day to be heard by God, or to get special favor from God, or to get some sort of heavenly merit, is an example of "meaningless repetition." Instead, our prayers should imitate that of Jesus before His heavenly Father, such as in John 17. However, we can and should pray for things more than one time—until we have the answer, or until we know that we have the answer and that no further prayer is needed, or until we have further insight into the will of God about the situation and know we are to pray differently. The Bible gives examples of Jesus (Mark 8:22-26; 14:35-39), the Apostle Paul (2 Corinthians 11:28; 12:8), and the disciples (Acts 12:3-6) doing this. In His ministry to a blind man, Jesus wanted to know if he had been healed, and then put His hands on the man again (Mark 8:25). Jesus did not tell the person to "confess that he was healed" or to "thank God for the healing," although there is a place for thanksgiving and the confession of faith (see the chapters on praise and Bible study). Jesus wanted an honest and specific appraisal of the person's health.

"And forgive us our debts, as we forgive our debtors" (Matthew 6:12)

The importance of forgiveness

Jesus taught that we must forgive. It is not optional. He connected forgiving others to prayer, to faith, and to receiving forgiveness (Matthew 6:12; 18:21-35, Mark 11:22-26). Briefly, there are four steps to forgiving others.

1. Confess to God that your anger, bitterness, unforgiveness, or hatred is sin.
2. As an act of your will (not emotions, which may still be hurt), forgive the person for their specific offenses. Pray out loud, "Father, as an act of my will, I forgive _____ for _____."

The Discipline of Intimacy

3. Ask God to bless that person, and renounce any curses against them (such as, "He took my candy—I hope he chokes on it!"). This includes resolving to not discuss that person's sin with others. If you cannot do this, you need to go back to steps 1 and 2.
4. Ask God to heal your heart.

"And do not lead us into temptation, but deliver us from the evil one"
(Matthew 6:13)

God desires that we walk in holiness

Holiness, which means purity and consecration, is to characterize our lives as God's people. As it is commanded in the New Testament (repeating a command in the Old Testament), "But as He who called you is holy, you also be holy in all your conduct, because it is written, 'Be holy, for I am holy'" (1 Peter 1:15-16). Victory over sin, avoiding temptation, and deliverance from evil are all part of the life of faith. It is only through faith we can please God (Hebrews 11:6). Our behavior will affect the lives of those around us, and it will ultimately determine our eternal reward (Revelation 20:12). The writer of Hebrews tells us that when we are struggling to overcome sin, "Let us therefore come boldly to the throne of grace, that we may obtain mercy and find grace to help in time of need," (Hebrews 4:16). As we dedicate ourselves to praying and forgiving as Jesus taught, we will find ourselves walking in holiness—and as we walk in holiness, we'll find ourselves more confident as we pray!

Praying the Scriptures

God has made promises (some of them are prophecies) that are recorded in the Bible. He is looking for people to ask Him to fulfill His promises (Ezekiel 22:30). God will keep His promises, but He is giving us an opportunity to be His co-workers—to work with Him, by praying, to bring His promises to fruition.

Jeremiah prophesied the destruction of Jerusalem, and said it would last 70 years. Then roughly that many years later, Daniel "understood by the books the number of the years specified by the word of the Lord through Jeremiah the prophet, that He would accomplish seventy years in the desolations of Jerusalem" (Daniel 9:2). Importantly, Daniel's response to that realization was to pray. "Then I set my face toward the Lord God to make request by prayer and supplications, with fasting, sackcloth, and ashes" (Daniel 9:3). God answered Daniel's prayer, and Jerusalem was rebuilt.

Psalm 122:6-7 gives these instructions on how to pray for Jerusalem: "Pray for the peace of Jerusalem: 'May they prosper who love you. Peace be within your walls, prosperity within your palaces.'" This may have been one of Daniel's life-long prayers. His habit was to pray three times a day. "Now when Daniel knew that the writing was signed, he went home. And in his upper room, with his windows open toward Jerusalem, he knelt down on his knees three times that day, and prayed and gave thanks before his God, as was his custom since early days" (Daniel 6:10).

It is clear that we are living in the last days before the return of Christ. We have an opportunity to participate in the timing of that event by sharing our faith, by walking in holiness, and by praying for the Lord's return. "Therefore, since all these things will be dissolved, what manner of persons ought you to be in holy conduct and godliness, looking for and hastening the coming of the day of God, because of which the heavens will be dissolved, being on fire, and the elements will melt with fervent heat?" (2 Peter 3:11-12). That is one prophecy we should pray for ("Come, Lord Jesus!"). As you find Bible verses that refer to other things that have not yet happened, make them a subject of regular prayer!

Suggestions for Our Individual Prayer Time

Time: It is good to have a set time devoted to prayer. For most people, morning is best. If you are most alert in the evening, that's fine, but be careful that you do not delay until you are too tired

Place: Find a particular place where you can be alone (so you can talk without concern about being heard by

The Discipline of Intimacy

others, so you can feel free to be open and honest with God). This can be a room, a place in the woods, or even in a car or on a walk.

Notes: Have a pen and paper available (or know how to use your phone or tablet to take notes), so that you can write down any ideas or convictions that come into your mind. Perhaps the Lord will speak to you, or you may think of something that you must do today. Instead of thinking of this constantly lest you forget to do it, write it down, so you can keep your attention focused on prayer. Then, get back to praying!

Bible: Pray the Word of God. When you read an instruction in the Bible, such as "be filled with the Spirit" (Ephesians 5:18), pray, "Father, help me to be filled with the Spirit."

"Watch": If you easily fall asleep while you are praying, do something to stay awake, such as walking, shouting, or even eating or drinking coffee. (These two are last resorts—if you are that sleepy, then you probably need to change your schedule!)

Diary: Have a notebook or prayer diary. Write down specific prayers, what God speaks to you, and the date. There may be times when you do not feel the Lord's presence as strongly as at other times. Continue to pray at these times especially, as the Scripture promises that we will reap what we sow (Galatians 6:7-9). A prayer notebook or diary can help us to keep our focus. It can provide a foundation for future prayers or ministry emphasis. Use the prayer notebook to record answers to prayer. You'll be able to look back and see what the Lord has done!

Listen: Spend some time, after you feel that you are in God's presence, simply being quiet, listening for God's voice. This is called waiting on the Lord (Psalm 85:8, Ecclesiastes 5:1). If God speaks to you, or if you have a vision or impression, pray according to those words, vision, or impression (see John 5:19-20; 8:38). For example, if you are thinking of someone and a picture of him falling into a hole comes to your mind, pray, "Father, protect him from evil plans, or from any traps that await him."

Maps: Maps can be very helpful if you are praying for the nations, as can literature on world geography.

A Sample Prayer Time

1. Begin with thanksgiving, praise, and worship.

   "Father, thank you for this day. Thank you for the safe trip we had yesterday. Thank you for the rain we have had recently. Let Your name be praised today. Be glorified in my life today!"

2. If you become aware of sins you have not yet confessed or have not already repented from, repent now!

   "Father, forgive me for my selfish attitude yesterday when I was talking with Mark. Forgive me for being critical of other saints and speaking against brother James."

3. Ask God what is on His heart.

   "Lord, I want Your kingdom to come and Your will to be done. What is on Your heart today?"

4. Wait on the Lord (be silent for some time, perhaps 30 seconds, but no more than a few minutes).

5. Pray for whatever the Lord speaks.

   "Father, I just had an impression that our neighbor is very upset about his car. Please give him peace, and wisdom about what to do. Use this problem to open his heart to the gospel."

6. Pray for wisdom for leaders—city, state, country, and international.

   "Father, I come before you on behalf of the president. Please give him wisdom and the fear of God as he leads this nation. Protect

him and his family from every evil influence. Give him grace to make right decisions."

7. Pray for the needs of the local church.

   "Jesus, You are building Your church. Give our elders wisdom as they lead us. Show them any new direction we may need at this time. Help sister Mary as she takes care of her mother."

8. Pray for the needs of the world—famines, disasters, and other prayers similar to the above. Tell the Lord what is on your heart.
9. Pray for the gospel to advance in the nations (Colossians 4:3).
10. Pray for Israel (Psalm 122:6-9).
11. Pray especially for your family—for salvation, healing, provision, and protection. (That's part of "give us this day our daily bread.")
12. Pray for those things the Lord has made you responsible for: your extended family, your friends, and work.
13. Pray for success in whatever is on your schedule for the day.
14. Pray for protection from temptation.
15. Thank the Lord for what you know He is going to do!

Group Prayer

The Bible makes particular mention of believers praying together (Acts 1:14; 2:42; 4:24-31). Because group prayer is so powerful, it is worthwhile making a few suggestions to facilitate believers praying together. There is a blessing of the Lord on unity.

> *Behold, how good and how pleasant it is*
> *For brethren to dwell together in unity!*
> *It is like the precious oil upon the head,*
> *Running down on the beard,*
> *The beard of Aaron,*
> *Running down on the edge of his garments.*
> *It is like the dew of Hermon,*

Descending upon the mountains of Zion;
For there the LORD commanded the blessing—
Life forevermore.

Psalm 133:1-3

The key to the special power of group prayer appears to be **agreement.** "Again I say to you that if two of you agree on earth concerning anything that they ask, it will be done for them by My Father in heaven. For where two or three are gathered together in My name, I am there in the midst of them" (Matthew 18:19-20).

This kind of prayer is to be purposeful and powerful. Scripture uses the illustration of a battle. If one can chase 1,000, then two can chase 10,000 (Deuteronomy 32:30). In practice, it might be that one person prays out loud, and the others say, "Amen!" It may seem simple and insignificant, but in fact this is so important that one of the names of the Lord is actually, "The Amen" (Revelation 3:14). The prayer that is spoken in a group must be clear, understandable, and one that each person praying can completely agree with. Tongues are not forbidden at prayer meetings, but the prayer of agreement must be in an understandable language (1 Corinthians 14:16-17). Practically speaking, these prayers should be brief and specific, so that there is no confusion, and everyone will be able to agree. For example, in Acts 4:24-30, they prayed for boldness and miracles, and that is exactly what they received: "Now, Lord, look on their threats, and grant to Your servants that with all boldness they may speak Your word, by stretching out Your hand to heal, and that signs and wonders may be done through the name of Your holy Servant Jesus. And when they had prayed, the place where they were assembled together was shaken; and they were all filled with the Holy Spirit, and they spoke the word of God with boldness," (Acts 4:29-31).

One person can pray out loud, and the others can say, "Amen!" It may seem simple and insignificant, but in fact this is so important that one of the names of the Lord is actually, "The Amen" (Revelation 3:14).

To use another "battle" illustration, if an army wishes to take control of a mountain top occupied by the enemy, an effective way to do this is to surround the mountain and advance on all sides at once, rather than sending up one soldier at a time. In a prayer meeting, if the Holy Spirit is leading the group to pray for a certain situation, each person who wants to pray for that situation should have a chance to do so before the group changes to a different subject. For example, if people are praying for the president, one person can pray (while the others agree) for wisdom for the president, someone else can pray for the president's protection, his family, etc. If one person prays for wisdom for the president, then someone prays for China, then someone prays for her neighbor's grandmother, it becomes more difficult to focus the group's attention on one subject and to wait on the Lord for what He might speak regarding how to pray for that subject.

Pray often with other believers, whether the gathering is called a "prayer meeting" or just a time of fellowship (Acts 2:42,46). A final word of guidance, however, is that a man and a woman who are not married to each other should avoid having private prayer meetings together for two reasons: to avoid temptation (2 Timothy 2:22 tells us to flee lust) and to avoid the appearance of evil (1 Thessalonians 5:22).

2. Fasting
The Discipline of Privation

Fasting means going without food or water or both. It is mentioned several times in both the Old and New Testaments, with an entire chapter (Isaiah 58) devoted to the subject. We will address why we should fast, some Scriptural examples of fasting, what happens to our bodies when we fast, the different kinds of fasts, and how to fast.

Why Fast?

Jesus Himself taught His disciples about fasting. In Matthew 6:16, He said, "When you fast…" He did not say, "If you fast," but "When you fast." Fasting is to be a part of the spiritual life of believers.

> *Is this not the fast that I have chosen: To loose the bonds of wickedness, to undo the heavy burdens, to let the oppressed go free, and that you break every yoke? Is it not to share your bread with the hungry, and that you bring to your house the poor who are cast out; when you see the naked, that you cover him, and not hide yourself from your own flesh? Then your light shall break forth like the morning, your healing shall spring forth speedily, and your righteousness shall go before you; the glory of the Lord shall be your rear guard. then you shall call, and the Lord will answer; You shall cry, and He will say, 'Here I am.' 'If you take away the yoke from your midst, the pointing of the finger, and speaking wickedness, if you extend your soul to the hungry and satisfy the afflicted soul, then your light shall dawn in the darkness, and your darkness shall be as the noonday. The Lord will guide you continually, and satisfy your soul in drought, and strengthen your bones; you shall be like a watered garden, and like a spring of water, whose waters do not fail. Those from among you shall build the old waste places; you shall raise up the foundations of many generations; and you shall be called the Repairer of the Breach, the Restorer of Streets to Dwell In.*

The Discipline of Privation

"If you turn away your foot from the Sabbath, from doing your pleasure on My holy day, and call the Sabbath a delight, the holy day of the lord honorable, and shall honor him, not doing your own ways, nor finding your own pleasure, nor speaking your own words, then you shall delight yourself in the Lord; and i will cause you to ride on the high hills of the earth, and feed you with the heritage of Jacob your father. The mouth of the Lord has spoken.

Isaiah 58:6-14

According to Isaiah 58, fasting can result in healing, righteousness (such as victory over sin or bad habits), and protection (v.8); it can lead to answered prayer (v.9), light (in other words, clarity or assurance of which way to go, what path to take, v.10), guidance, satisfaction, and strength (v.11), as well as restoration and effective ministry (v.12). For example, the men of Jabesh Gilead fasted seven days after Israel had been defeated in battle, and this marked a turning point in the history of their nation (1 Samuel 31:13). Daniel 10 describes an angelic messenger from God that overcame demonic interference as an answer to three weeks of prayer and fasting. Jesus fasted for 40 days in the wilderness after being baptized, and returned in the power of the Spirit to begin His earthly ministry (Luke 4:14). Cornelius was fasting when an angel came with a message that enabled his household to become the first Gentiles to believe in Jesus as Lord and Savior and receive the Holy Spirit.

One word describes all those events: **Power!** Ultimately, this power accompanies or is released by fasting in a number of ways:

- Fasting can place us in a position to receive from God;
- It can disable the devil and cause a spiritual breakthrough;
- It helps us to focus our attention on the Lord and on the answer to our prayers;
- It denies our flesh;
- It builds our faith by ministering to our spirit and denying our flesh. In other words, it crosses our will: We want to eat, but when we fast, we are refusing our body's desire to eat.

Many people advocate fasting on the basis that it is good for our bodies. From a strictly medical view, it has been helpful to some people, but the evidence that it helps everyone is unconvincing. As Christians, our choice to fast should ultimately be based on the fact that it is within God's will for us to do so. Fasting will benefit us spiritually!

Some Scriptural Examples of Fasting

1. Deuteronomy 9:9,18 (also Exodus 24:12-18) - Twice, Moses went 40 days without food or water while he was in the presence of God on the mountain. This was a supernatural experience initiated by God. Moses did not decide to pray and seek the Lord and fast food and water for 40 days. God commanded Moses, "Come up to Me!" (Exodus 24:12). While in God's presence, water and food simply were not part of Moses' experience. As there is no way a man can survive 40 days without water, the experience must have included miraculous sustenance of Moses' life.

2. Judges 20:26 - The Israelites fasted after twice being defeated in battle. The result was a victory in the third battle.

3. 1 Samuel 7:5-6 - The Israelites combined fasting with confession and repentance.

4. Psalm 35:13 - David combined fasting with prayer for the sick.

5. Psalm 69:10 - David used fasting as a way to chasten his soul.

6. Isaiah 58:3-5 - In addition to listing the benefits of fasting, this chapter also talks about an "incorrect" fast, when people were fasting to be "religious" (in other words, they had a wrong attitude—one of appearing to be devout, but with no inward change of heart). Verses 6 to 14 describe instead "the fast that God has chosen": to stop oppressing others, to deny ourselves, and to share.

7. Daniel 9:1-3,21 - Daniel fasted and prayed as he sought God to fulfill Jeremiah's prophecy and restore Jerusalem.

8. Jonah 3:5-10 - The people of Nineveh repented at the preaching of Jonah, and this was accompanied by crying "mightily to God" (verse 8) and by "man and beast" fasting (that is, abstaining from) both food and water.

9. Matthew 4:1-2 (also Luke 4:2) - Jesus fasted for 40 days. Although it does not say whether He drank water, it may be assumed that He did for two reasons. First, it says he was hungry. If a person goes without food and water for just a few days, he will desire water before food. Since Scripture describes only His hunger, we can conclude that He had water during these 40 days. Second, Jesus fasted while being tempted by the devil (Luke 4:2). In other words, He was doing this as a Man, with the weaknesses that characterize our humanity (yet without sin). To survive 40 days without water clearly requires Divine intervention (for example, like that which enabled Moses to survive without water and food when he was on the mountain of God), which would make dealing with temptation less meaningful.

10. Matthew 17:14-21 - Jesus mentions prayer and fasting as the means to release the spiritual power needed for a particular kind of deliverance.

11. Acts 13:1-3 - The Holy Spirit spoke to the disciples as they were "ministering to the Lord and fasting." Fasting again accompanied sending out Paul and Barnabas on their apostolic journey.

What Happens To Our Bodies When We Fast

Normally, our bodies use a type of sugar called glucose for energy. This glucose circulates in our blood, and enables our muscles to pull, our brain to think, and our heart to beat. For the first 24 to 48 hours without food, our bodies use a special form of glucose called glycogen, which is stored in the liver. After this is exhausted, the body must convert other compounds in the body to glucose, and begins to use the energy stored in fat. However, it takes the body from several days to two weeks to adapt to using fat as an energy source. (The switch from using glucose to fatty acids is similar to converting a gasoline engine to using another fuel—it takes some time, and until all the necessary changes are made, there is an inefficient use of fuel.) After this period, the brain becomes accustomed to functioning on fatty acids, although it may not function as well as it previously did on glucose (especially noticeable in situations where "quick thinking" is necessary). This continues until almost all the fat in the body is depleted. The length of time until this happens depends on an individual's height, weight (especially the amount of fat they have), metabolism, activity, and environmental temperature. During a fast, one may notice that he (or she) gets dizzy when standing up, that his breath has a peculiar odor, and that he feels weaker, colder, and sleepier than usual (although he may not be able to actually sleep well). Some find themselves daydreaming more when they fast. Sometimes people feel achy "in their bones." Some people experience headaches for the first day or two of a fast, especially if they are accustomed to consuming caffeine (such as that contained in coffee, tea, cola and similar soft drinks, and chocolate). After most of the fat in the body is gone, the body comes to a place of actual starvation—which means that it does not have enough energy to survive, and it must destroy essential tissue to make energy. This may be what is referred to when Jesus fasted, and **afterward** became hungry (Matthew 4:2).

Kinds of Fasts

Although it does not actually give them specific names, the Bible does mention different kinds of fasts, and it can be helpful for us to use labels in order to discuss and understand each one better.

1. An **absolute fast** is one in which nothing is consumed—no food or water. Prolonged absolute fasting is mentioned in the Bible only when there was a miraculous event enabling the people involved to survive. Otherwise, it was only for brief periods (up to three days).
2. A **normal fast** is to consume only water.
3. A **partial fast** is any fast in which some foods or drinks (other

than water) are taken. Daniel 10:3 describes such a fast, in which Daniel denied himself any food that he enjoyed, specifically no meat or wine. (Many people refer to that as a "vegetable fast" or "fasting meats and dessert.") Some people have felt led by the Lord to eat only certain foods, or juices, or vegetables, while others only deny themselves certain foods, such as desserts or chocolates.

Suggestions for How to Fast

As Jesus mentioned in Matthew 6:16-18, fasting is to be done before God. Therefore, when we fast, it is a choice made freely in light of our relationship with the Lord (that is, whatever we feel the Lord leading us to not eat or drink, when and for how long, and for what reasons). What makes the fast acceptable to God is the self-denial and righteous actions which reflect a proper heart attitude of humility and contrition before God (Isaiah 58). Indeed, Jesus warned against fasting simply for the purpose of drawing others' attention. If we are fasting, especially for long periods, others will know (and some will need to know). For example, it is perfectly reasonable to tell your wife that you are fasting. This is not so that you can impress her with how spiritual you are, but so that she does not unnecessarily prepare food. Additionally, if someone finds out that you are fasting, that does not mean your fast becomes useless. Jesus was talking about our *motive* for fasting. If we fast for God and not for men, whether or not people find out about it is irrelevant.

It is usually easier to fast if you decide beforehand how long the fast will be. If you have never fasted before, start with a short fast. Begin by fasting only one meal or one day (unless the Lord has spoken to you to fast longer), drinking only water. Once you are able to go one day without food, you may want to try a longer period with only water, or with water and juices or vegetables. Use common sense! Be wise when you are fasting. If you do construction work on skyscrapers, for example, and you get dizzy when you fast, then either do not fast when you are working or eat whatever is necessary to allow you to work safely (see 1 Corinthians 7:22 and

2 Corinthians 8:12). If you find yourself in a communion service during a fast, feel free to partake, unless you specifically feel that the Lord wants you to refrain. You only need a tiny amount of food to "proclaim the Lord's death till He comes" (1 Corinthians 11:26).

It is important to take time for prayer during a fast. Often, the Lord will have us fast for a particular purpose, and in the act of fasting we can seek Him and pray for His will to be done in that situation. If you are facing an important decision and need clear guidance from the Lord, fasting and prayer is a great way to clear your mind to hear from the Lord: During the fast, use the "extra" time (that is, the time you normally would spend on meal preparation and eating) to pray and read the Bible, listening to the Lord and searching the Scriptures for direction. If you find yourself in a challenging situation and you suspect there are demonic forces at work, prayer and fasting can be effective tools to bring about a breakthrough. I heard a man tell of how, as a young man, he worked in a home for troubled and disabled children. One severely autistic child had something about him that made this man suspect that demons were affecting the child—either causing the child's condition or somehow tormenting the child. The man had not been a Christian very long, but after reading Matthew 17:21, he decided to go on an extended fast (several weeks), fasting and praying specifically for the child's deliverance. On the last day of the fast, as the man was holding the child in a rocking chair as he often did, he commanded the demons to leave the child. To the man's amazement, the child pulled away from him and seemed to fly or "levitate" all the way across the room into the opposite wall and collapsed! Three days later, the child was discharged from the facility, having become normal!

If you are drinking only water, then drink plenty of it, especially during a longer fast. Unless you have a clear, supernatural experience calling you to fast longer, do not continue an absolute fast beyond three days. Also, do not fast more than 40 days without a word from God. This is because a fast that lasts longer than 10 days is generally reserved for special times of drawing close to God. Depending on your physical condition (and fat reserves!), fasts longer than 30 or 35 days can actually be dangerous, so it is good to have "permission" from the Lord before fasting for that length of time. If, after a prolonged fast, you begin to feel pain in your stomach, or if you suddenly notice a marked change in how you feel overall, it is probably a signal that your body is running out of fat reserves and it is time to break your fast.

How often or how much to fast will depend on a number of factors, your particular responsibilities and circumstances being the most important--and so you fast in order to seek wisdom and the Lord's will within them. For example, if you are responsible for overseeing other individuals or a project, and a problem arises, you may wish to add fasting to the other actions you take to solve the problem, (such as fasting and praying for a person to be delivered, like is mentioned in Matthew 17:21.) In reading Matthew's account, it is interesting that Jesus did not immediately begin fasting when He encountered demonized (demon possessed) people; prayer and fasting were already part of His life. It was almost as if He had a "power tank" that He kept constantly full. If there are no pressing needs, you may feel that occasional or regular fasting keeps you more spiritually "fit": It is part of the process of "disciplining our bodies" (1 Corinthians 9:27). This may be especially important if you are or hope to be in Christian ministry (see Acts 13:2 and 2 Corinthians 6:5 and 11:27). For example, some individuals in ministry feel comfortable with fasting regularly, such as one or two days each week, or several days once a month. One minister used to speak of fasting 40 days twice every year! Not surprisingly, he had a powerful ministry.

Ending a Fast

It is wise to break a fast gradually. If you have been on a three day absolute fast, then start with just water (which you will want anyway), perhaps one or two glasses, followed by another about half an hour later. After a longer fast, your stomach shrinks somewhat, and the bacterial content of your intestines changes. It is good to begin eating small amounts of foods that are easily digested. First drink juices, then—perhaps the next meal—introduce starches (rice, bread, or boiled potatoes) and yogurt. The next meal or the next day, add lean meat, then fruits and vegetables, and lastly fatty foods and milk. If you quickly consume all the things you missed during the fast, you may have some severe "G.I. distress"!

A Note to Those Taking Medication

If you are on daily medication and plan to fast, consult the prescribing physician. Some doctors will regard fasting as unimportant or too dangerous and tell you not to fast. Actually, only very rarely does a medical condition preclude fasting, but fasting may make things more complicated. Some conditions and medications require no change at all with fasting. Ask your doctor how you can most safely fast (not if you can fast).

Summary

Fasting is to be part of the devotional life of every Christian. It is part of the process of self-denial that Jesus said His disciples were to practice. It is to be done in order to be noticed by God, not to impress people, and what food or beverage we abstain from is our decision to make (except when the Lord specifically tells us what to eat, drink, or abstain from). Absolute fasts (no food or water) should never be longer than three days. Spiritual growth and spiritual power, as well as answers to prayer, can be expected as we fast.

3. Bible Reading
The Discipline of Study

How the Bible was written

The Bible is a collection of 66 books: 39 in the Old Testament and 27 in the New Testament. These books were written by various authors over the course of about two thousand years, and they all share a central theme: God's relationship with man. The Bible is Truth in its entirety—every word. As holy men of God like Moses, David, or Jeremiah were moved by the Holy Spirit, they spoke the word of the Lord that was then passed down by scribes into the books of our Biblical cannon. Standards for copying the Scriptures (another name for the Bible) were incredibly strict. The scribes counted every letter, so that they even knew the middle letter of the Old Testament!

Some critics have tried to disparage the Bible by using examples like having people whisper something from one person to another. Often done in a classroom setting, the last person usually ends up hearing something completely different from the original word or statement started by the first person. Such "demonstrations" are misleading and even dishonest. Imagine how little difference there would be from the first to last person if the phrase were to be written down, proofread by the writer, the receiver, and a third party, and the letters were each numbered and verified with each transition! This is the process that the Scriptures underwent as they were passed down through the centuries.

The Old Testament was originally written in Hebrew, with a few pages in Chaldean. The New Testament was written in Greek (or possibly Hebrew, although most scholars say it was Greek), with a few Aramaic words. Bibles in modern languages are translated either from copies of Hebrew and Greek manuscripts, or simply from other translations. Some translations are the result of attempts to be literal and match the original style and wording as much as possible, while others paraphrase and convey the main meaning of each phrase or sentence, although individual words may not be translated exactly.

A concordance is an alphabetical listing of all the words in the Bible. It tells where in the Bible (which verse) each word is used. The sentences in the Bible have been numbered. They are called verses, and are usually designated by book, chapter, and number. Some concordances also give the original Hebrew or Greek word. Bible apps are available that can instantly show the original word (in Hebrew or Greek) that the modern word was translated from.

Ultimately, the words of the Bible are God's words. They are His messages and truth to people, revealing Himself or His ways or His will to them. The actual paper and ink are only paper and ink, nothing more. Bibles themselves (i.e., the paper and ink that comprise the book) have no magical qualities. (However, some people of other faiths consider the Bible, including the physical pages and cover, as a holy book, even though they may be convinced the Bible has been corrupted. Seeing a Christian putting a Bible on the floor or treating it with apparent disrespect by tossing it onto a sofa or table may be offensive to them in light of their religious background.) Simply having a Bible in a room, house, coffin, or anywhere else has no special power, nor does it win favor or merit from God.

Parts of the Bible

1. Moses wrote the first five books of the Bible: Genesis ("the book of beginnings"), Exodus, Leviticus, Numbers, and Deuteronomy. These are also collectively called the Pentateuch, the Law, or the Torah.

2. The Pentateuch is followed by a series of books detailing Jewish history after the time of Moses until about 350 years BC. These are the historical books, which include Joshua, Judges, Ruth, 1 and 2 Samuel, 1 and 2 Kings, 1 and 2 Chronicles, Ezra, Nehemiah, and Esther.

3. Next are the poetical books (although they do not rhyme): Job (which deals with the question of why the righteous

suffer), Psalms (a collection of songs, emphasizing man's relationship with God), Proverbs (wisdom sayings for man's relationship with other people), Ecclesiastes (the observations of a wise man regarding earthly life, especially life apart from a relationship with God), and the Song of Solomon (a song with the theme of romantic love, it also is an allegory of the relationship of Christ and the church).

4. A series of books by the Hebrew prophets then follows the poetical books. They are divided into what are called the Major Prophets (Isaiah, Jeremiah, Lamentations, Ezekiel, Daniel) and the Minor Prophets (Hosea, Joel, Amos, Obadiah, Jonah, Micah, Nahum, Habakkuk, Zephaniah, Haggai, Zechariah, Malachi).

5. The New Testament begins with the four Gospels (Matthew, Mark, Luke, John). Written by those of their namesakes, the Gospels record the life and ministry of Jesus Christ.

6. The Acts of the Apostles, or Acts, as it is usually known, follows the four Gospels. It is an account of the beginning of the Christian Church.

7. After Acts, there are a number of letters (or "epistles"). These are written by early Church leaders to individuals, churches, and to the Jewish Christians. They contain doctrines (teachings) of the Christian faith and many specific applications of Christ's teachings to daily life.

8. The last book in the Bible is Revelation. This is a very dramatic series of visions seen by the Apostle John, which contain glimpses of heaven, predictions about the end times, and reassurances of Christ's (and Christians') ultimate victory.

Other Writings

Under the leadership of the Holy Spirit, in the first centuries AD Christian churches and leaders reached an agreement about which writings were divinely inspired. Those writings were called the "Canon of Scripture." Another collection of religious writings was not accepted as Scripture. It is called the Apocrypha, and it is sometimes included in Orthodox and Catholic Bibles. Protestant translations do not usually include them. Although they have some literary and historical value, since they are not inspired by God, they have no authoritative value in Christian belief. It is best to not read them along with our daily Bible reading, lest we confuse or contaminate the "pure milk of the word" (1 Peter 2:2).

Unholy "Scriptures"

There are a few translations of the Bible that are not true to the original Scriptures. An example of such a translation is the one used by English speaking Jehovah's Witnesses. There are also other books that are carried, used, sold, and promoted by certain religions and sects that are likewise deviant from the Bible. Generally, we should not read these texts. Like the experts who learn to recognize counterfeit money by studying the genuine, we can better use our time studying the Bible, not the counterfeits. Examples of the texts that Christians should avoid are the Book of Mormon (used by the Mormons) and Watchtower Magazine (read by Jehovah's Witnesses).

Why Read the Bible?

Reading God's word is essential for spiritual growth. According to the Bible, the Scripture is inspired by God (2 Timothy 3:16); it is forever settled in heaven (Psalm 119:89); it won't fade away (Isaiah 40:8); it shows us how to live (Psalm 119:1); it makes us wise for salvation (2 Timothy 3:15); and reading it, meditating on it, and obeying it gives success and prosperity (Joshua 1:8). It offers certainty to knowing what God is speaking, and it is the ultimate judge of revelation. (In other words, any revelation must agree with the Bible; if it does not, the revelation is false.) The Bible is the only written authority for all matters of faith and practice.

"In the beginning was the Word, and the Word was with God, and the Word was God," (John 1:1). "Many nations shall come and say, 'Come, and let us go up to the mountain of the LORD, to the house of the God of Jacob; He will teach us His ways, and we shall walk in His paths.' For out of Zion the law shall go forth, and the word of the LORD from Jerusalem," (Micah 4:2). As we learn God's word, we get to know Jesus (the Word of God, John 1:1) better and we learn God's ways (Micah 4:2)—and this results in us walking in His paths (in other words, living and behaving like He wants us to).

How to Read the Bible

The Bible is meant to change our lives. Jesus said that man lives by every word that proceeds from the mouth of God (Matthew 4:4). Since the Bible is spiritual food, it is good to be familiar with the whole Bible. A recommended goal is to read the entire Bible once every year or two. To read the Bible in a year, we would need to read approximately four chapters each day, assuming some missed days. This is usually easier and more interesting if we read from several different sections of the Bible each day, rather than reading four chapters in a row. The eight parts of the Bible previously listed are not of equal length, so a good way to methodically cover the entire Bible is to read one chapter from the New Testament and three from the Old Testament (one chapter each from three of the four parts of the Old Testament) each day.

Some Suggestions for Bible Note-taking

Feel free to write notes in your Bible. Writing references to related verses can be very helpful. Writing the date you read a chapter or book can help to monitor progress on Bible reading. A pencil or a pen with a very fine tip is best for this particular purpose. Avoid ink and markers that penetrate through the paper!

It is helpful to have a notebook or a notes app (such as Evernote, OneNote, or whatever your favorite note-taking app is) of the subjects we have studied in the Bible, for future reference. Keep a notebook or app record of what is shared at church. When you hear a message in church, note the verses that are shared. Also, note any statements that are especially meaningful to you, or that you are not sure are true. Later, study what you heard. Look up the verses and try to find verses that will support what the preacher has shared. If you hear something that is clearly incorrect, locate verses to prove it. Know what you believe! What we are taught must be real in our hearts if it is to benefit us.

Studying the Bible

Experience the Word! Look up verses to meet your needs, to solve problems, and to explain unusual experiences. For example, if Jehovah's Witnesses come to your door, 2 John 10-11 instructs that you are to not let them into your house. (If you want to share the gospel with them, do it outside!) Or, if you meet someone who proclaims reincarnation, Hebrews 9:27 teaches us that we die only once, and after that comes judgment. When we study the Bible, we have the liberty of studying "by the Spirit." Being familiar with the Bible will help us other ways as well, like in the ability to judge dreams and visions. If we remember a dream, we can then study the Bible to learn the symbolic meaning of things in the dream.

If you do not understand a verse, memorize it! The Lord will open your eyes to the meaning of verses as you go through further experiences of life and Christian growth. Jesus said, "If anyone wants to do His will, he shall know concerning the doctrine, whether it is from God or whether I speak on My own authority," (John 7:17). If you want to know a doctrine or Scripture, decide to do the word. Obey what the Bible teaches, even if (or especially if) it makes you uncomfortable or requires you to change.

If you ever feel like something the Bible is teaching you to do "feels wrong," you may be misunderstanding what is written. (For example, some people have misinterpreted Mark 16:18 to mean they should intentionally handle poisonous snakes.) If you find yourself in this situation, get together with one or more mature believers to help you understand what the Bible says.

As we study the Bible, we can focus on books, characters, authors (for example, all the writings of the Apostle John), subjects, time

The Discipline of Study

periods, or the usage of particular words. The goal of study should be a greater knowledge of the truth (the Bible), so that we can then have a greater revelation of the ultimate Truth (Jesus Christ). Using 1 Corinthians 11:27 as an example, we will demonstrate what to look at when examining a verse:

"Therefore whoever eats this bread or drinks this cup of the Lord in an unworthy manner will be guilty of the body and blood of the Lord," (1 Corinthians 11:27).

The context. Ask yourself:

When was this written?
The first century after Christ's death.

Who wrote this?
The Apostle Paul and brother Sosthenes (1 Corinthians 1:1).

To whom was this written?
To the believers in the Corinthian Church (1 Corinthians 1:2).

What is the subject of this book?
Avoiding carnality in the church. Specific problems such as divisions, immorality, and disorder are addressed.

What is the subject of this chapter?
Certain traditions Paul had taught the Corinthians, specifically head coverings and Communion.

What is the subject of the preceding and following verses?
The proper way and significance of taking communion (verses 17-34).

The intent. Ask yourself:

Why was this written?
There was commotion and disorder at church meetings.

Was there a specific problem?
Yes, people were getting drunk and eating without consideration of others at communion services (1 Corinthians 11:21).

Is there a universal interest being addressed?

Chapter 3: Bible Reading

Yes, the meaning of Communion (verses 23-26), and the importance of order in Communion (verses 27-34).

What was the author trying to accomplish when he wrote this?
He wanted the Corinthians to correct the way they took Communion.

Was he trying to instruct to give better understanding of doctrine?
Yes, he was instructing them on the symbolism and meaning of Communion.

The meaning. Ask yourself:

What is the apparent meaning?
Do not demean communion. Be polite and wait for each other.

Is there a deeper, less obvious meaning?
Communion is serious, meaningful, and powerful. We need to take communion in a worthy manner. This includes the necessity of being born again (verse 29), having a clear conscience (verse 28), and having no unconfessed or ongoing sin (verse 31).

Is there any symbolic meaning?
The bread and wine represent the body and blood of the Lord.

Which is more important, the literal meaning(s), or the symbolic meaning(s)?
In this case, they are both significant.

Are there any key words or phrases that point to the meaning? (Hint: Two important things to watch for are key words, such as therefore, so that, etc., and the first time a word or idea is used, which is often introduced as far back as Genesis.)
Yes, the word "therefore" (verses 27 & 33).

The application. Ask yourself:

How would application of this verse affect life in the twenty-first century?
Taking communion probably was different then than in most churches today. It seems to have included more of a meal than just one small piece of bread and a sip of wine or grape juice.

How does this verse apply to my life?
Its main application is in the context of communion.

Does my life (my thoughts, words, actions) measure up to what this verse requires?
If you hide things you have done or are doing from God, then you are falling short.

Do I need to change to fully obey or fulfill this verse?
If you tend to be inconsiderate of other Christians, or if you treat communion as any common meal, or if you hold on to sin in your life, you need to change.

Resources

There are a number of helpful resources in studying the Bible. Many are now available online or as apps (for example, BibleGateway, YouVersion, etc.). Concordances (which are found in the back of some Bibles) list the words used in the Bible and where they are found. Lexicons (which may be included in "exhaustive" concordances) define the ancient Hebrew and Greek words. Bible dictionaries give the meaning of the words in the Bible. Bible encyclopedias are usually multiple volume works that cover almost every subject in the Bible in considerable detail. Bible handbooks are single volume editions with brief studies on the more important Bible subjects. Bible commentaries try to give the meanings and interpretations of the Scriptures, book by book or verse by verse. Finally, a Bible Atlas has maps marking places mentioned in the Bible. These resources are useful both alone and in conjunction with each other; for example, a dictionary will define what prophecy is, while an encyclopedia will have a four-page discussion of prophecy, with corresponding scriptures and possibly the inclusion of research results on how prophecy itself was viewed in ancient times. A handbook will have a few paragraphs on prophecy and several Scripture references, but a commentary may mention a specific prophecy in its discussion of a chapter. Although these resources are valuable, make sure to not substitute them for your own Bible reading!

Chapter 3: Bible Reading

Meditating On Scripture

We are taught to meditate on the Bible (Joshua 1:8). This has nothing to do with "Eastern" meditation! Meditating on Scripture is to think about the meanings and applications of a particular verse. We first memorize a portion of Scripture. Then, we think about each word and phrase. The following is a sample meditation of John 3:16:

"For God so loved": This tells us that God is able to love, and that He loved very much.

"the world": God loves everyone. He loves everyone a lot.

"that He gave": God's love caused Him to take action. It was not just an emotion. In fact, this love is nothing like the romantic lust in books, movies, TV, and the Internet. The love of God motivated Him to give.

"His only begotten Son": How great was this love! What a tremendous sacrifice. Imagine giving an only son! The feelings in the heart of God the Father must be very similar to our own feelings toward our children. This is amazing.

"that whoever": This means all people—everywhere.

"believes in Him": The key is to believe, to have faith. This means that believing has eternal consequences. Faith must be life changing. It is not vague or without direction. It must be faith in Jesus Christ! Taken in context with the rest of the New Testament, "believe" includes both repentance and faith.

"should not perish": Some people will perish. Eternal damnation is a reality. But God does not want people to perish eternally. He wants people to be in heaven, not in torment.

"but have everlasting life": There is an afterlife or age to come. The alternative to perishing is to have life. This life is everlasting, and we can choose to enter into this life by believing in the Son of God.

The Discipline of Study

Memorizing

Memorizing Scripture is easier than it seems. First, choose a verse or chapter to memorize that is meaningful to you. Copy the Scripture onto a card or paper that you can carry in your pocket or purse, or have it come up readily on a smartphone. Write the reference (for example, "John 3:16") above and below the Scripture. Whenever you have a moment, look at the words. Waiting (in lines, for elevators, etc.) is a great time for this. Each time you review a verse, repeat the reference before and after the verse. When you can repeat the entire verse without looking, you can begin to meditate on it, and begin to memorize another verse! Memorizing and meditating on Scriptures can ultimately help to heal people's minds, especially those with past drug or alcohol abuse. As our thoughts begin to coincide with God's word, our minds will become more orderly and centered on Him.

Once we believe and know God's word, we can also speak it. ("Speak it," means "quote it," but not as if we are repeating something for a Sunday School class prize, identifying the reference after quoting the words. Speak the phrase or sentence to or about a situation!) This is very important, as the spoken word releases special power "But what does it say? 'The word is near you, in your mouth and in your heart' (that is, the word of faith which we preach): that if you confess with your mouth the Lord Jesus and believe in your heart that God has raised Him from the dead, you will be saved. For with the heart one believes unto righteousness, and with the mouth confession is made unto salvation," (Romans 10:8-10; see also Mark 11:23, Romans 10:17, and 2 Corinthians 4:13).

When you encounter a difficult or unusual situation, ask God to show you the appropriate Bible verse, and then apply the word of God to that situation. For example, speak the word out loud. (See John chapter 11 for an example of Jesus doing this.)

Read, study, memorize, meditate on, and quote the Scriptures! As we do that, we grow in our knowledge of Jesus Christ and of God's ways we think and behave more like Jesus, our minds are healed and strengthened, and we receive joy and other blessings from God.

4. Praise
The Discipline of Adoration

What Praise Is

Praise is telling God how great He is. It is the natural response of every created being as we truly recognize our Creator God. David, the shepherd who killed Goliath and later became king of Israel, had a unique understanding of praise. He wrote many of the Psalms, which are filled with instructions and examples of praise. David's order of praise and thanksgiving even served as the model used by subsequent kings of Israel (2 Chronicles 7:6; 8:14; 23:18). The New Testament also has examples of praise, such as numerous descriptions of praise even in heaven itself. However, instead of giving more instructions about how to praise, the New Testament usually refers back to the Psalms.

In his letter to the Ephesians, the Apostle Paul offers a command to believers: "And do not be drunk with wine, in which is dissipation; but be filled with the Spirit, speaking to one another in psalms and hymns and spiritual songs, singing and making melody in your heart to the Lord, giving thanks always for all things to God the Father in the name of our Lord Jesus Christ," (Ephesians 5:18-20). We are to be filled with the Spirit and sing psalms! Colossians 3:16 tells us to let the word of God dwell in us richly and to sing psalms. If singing psalms is related to being filled with the Spirit and the word of God, it must be very important. We are to do everything to the glory of God (1 Corinthians 10:31), and whoever offers praise glorifies God (Psalm 50:23). God must be praised! That is not an exhortation; it is an eternal truth based on God's character. Referring to those who praised Him as He rode into Jerusalem, Jesus said, "If these should keep silent, the stones would immediately cry out" (Luke 19:40). In heaven itself, the seraphim do not cease saying, "Holy, holy, holy, Lord God Almighty, Who was and is and is to come!" while the elders repeatedly fall down and worship before Him (Revelation 4:8-11).

Ultimately, praise depends upon God's greatness, and not upon our voice quality, musical talent, instruments, emotions, or circumstances. Since God has ordained for us to praise Him (Psalm 81:1-5), we should praise Him as He commands us. We are to praise God His way, not our way. He is our King and Lord, we are His people. We are to praise the Lord all the time (Psalm 34:1), every day (Psalm 145:2), in all nations (Psalm 57:9), with our whole heart (Psalm 138:1), according to His righteousness (Psalm 7:17), and according to His greatness (Psalm 150:2). Psalm 100:4 says to enter God's gates with thanksgiving and His courts with praise. This is one reason we often begin church meetings with singing.

The Psalmist exclaims of the Lord, "But You are holy, enthroned in the praises of Israel," (Psalm 22:3). In this verse, "enthroned" can be translated "dwelling" or "inhabiting": God inhabits the praises of Israel—God lives in the praises of His people! When we praise the Lord, we draw close to Him, and He draws close to us (James 4:8). As a result, it is also good to begin devotional time with the Lord through thanksgiving and praise, as it opens our hearts to allow a greater closeness with Him.

Praise and Spiritual Warfare

In parallel to its place of worship unto God, praise is a powerful weapon in spiritual warfare. As the Israelites went into battle against the Ammonites, Moabites, and the inhabitants of Mount Seir, King Jehoshaphat placed the singers and those responsible of praise in front of the armed warriors (2 Chronicles 20:21)! The result was a great victory for Israel. When Paul and Silas were beaten and jailed, they were singing hymns at midnight. God was listening, and an earthquake released the apostles from their chains, which ultimately led to the jailer and his household being saved by believing in Jesus Christ (Acts 16:25-34). In praise, we have the honor of binding our spiritual enemies (Psalm 149:6-9, Isaiah 30:32).

Before listing specific instructions about praise, it is worth noting what the Bible does not say. It does not include any musical notes or scales, nor does it forbid any musical instrument. The Bible never says that listening to music is praising God. It also does not promote or forbid any particular type of music, although some music can be corrupted by the devil (Ezekiel 28:13). If it excites our carnality, or if it is painfully loud, or if the attention is on the music or the musicians and not on the Lord, then it is appropriate to consider it unwholesome.

Unfortunately, some musical styles that convey themes of frustration, anger, and violence are simply inappropriate. If that is what you love to listen to, deliverance from bondage may be needed.

Specific Instructions

1. Sing the kind of praise songs you enjoy singing. Praise should be pleasant (Psalm 147:1).

2. Do not be afraid to make up a new melody and new words. Psalm 33:3 tells us to "Sing to Him a new song; play skillfully with a shout of joy" As we do this at the leading of the Holy Spirit, this can take the form of prophecies, songs, and singing in tongues (1 Corinthians 14:15). This is sometimes referred to as "the song of the Lord." If you want to remember a song the Lord gives you, a recording app or sound recorder is helpful, unless you are skillful at writing music and choose to instead save it this way.

3. Clap your hands (Psalm 47:1).

4. Dance to the Lord (Psalm 30:11; 149:3; 150:4, 1 Samuel 6:14, Exodus 15:20, 1 Chronicles 15:29). This dancing can be organized, or it can be hopping or jumping up and down as the Holy Spirit moves our hearts. It is not disco dancing or waltzing, and it is absolutely never sensuous or suggestive, nor does it ever involve a man and a woman embracing. Instead, it is a time of intimacy with the Lord in worship. It should not become a distraction to the greater worship in a meeting.

5. Praise loudly (2 Chronicles 30:21, Luke 19:37).

6. Praise with "a ringing cry" or a shout of joy (Psalm 32:11; 35:27).

7. Praise with a shout (Psalm 47:1).
8. Praise with singing (Psalm 30:4).
9. Praise with hymns (Matthew 26:30).
10. Praise with zeal, and gloriously (Psalm 66:2).
11. Praise with instruments:
    a. Cymbals (Psalm 150:5),
    b. Flutes (Psalm 87:7; 150:4),
    c. Harp (Psalm 49:4; 57:8; 71:22),
    d. Harp of 10 strings (Psalm 33:2; 144:9),
    e. Lute (Psalm 33:2; 57:8),
    f. Horn (Psalm 47:5; 81:3; 98:6),
    g. Strings (Psalm 150:4),
    h. Timbrel or tambourine (Psalm 81:2; 149:3), and
    i. Skillfully (Psalm 33:3).

As Christians, we are to put on "a garment of praise" instead of "the spirit of heaviness" (Isaiah 61:3). Satan wants us to be discouraged, because the "joy of the Lord is your strength" (Nehemiah 8:10). Deciding to praise the Lord is an act of our will. King David even commanded his own soul to bless the Lord, as if he was giving orders to a soldier: "Bless the LORD, O my soul; and all that is within me, bless His holy name! Bless the LORD, O my soul, and forget not all His benefits," (Psalm 103:1-2). When we praise the Lord and focus on Him, we necessarily take our attention off ourselves and our situations. That alone can be enough to set us free from discouragement and depression! As Corrie ten Boom used to say, "Look around, and be distressed; look within, and be depressed; look at Jesus, and be at rest!"

Suggestions for Praise

When you come to informal church gatherings, have a song or two on your heart to suggest or to start singing (depending on the format or usual flow of the meeting). When you are praising the Lord, keep your mind off everything else. Praising is an important ministry to the Lord; it is our opportunity to bless Him. He deserves our very best, our undivided attention. If you play an instrument, practice praising the Lord using your instrument. If possible, bring it to church. If you do not play an instrument, you might consider learning to play a simple one, such as guitar, tambourine, ukulele, castanets, or even spoons.

Praise is both commanded by the Lord and is a normal response to the greatness of God. It is one of the keys to a healthy devotional life and to growing in Christ. Singing the praises of God (in other words, setting praise to music) is described in considerable detail in the Psalms, and can involve virtually any instrument or musical style. It is a powerful weapon in spiritual warfare. Praise ushers in the presence of the Lord, and praising God can break the power of heaviness and depression in our lives.

5. Witnessing
The Discipline of Compassion

Sharing our faith with others is one of the most rewarding and challenging experiences of following Christ. Jesus said, "Come after Me, and I will make you become fishers of men," (Mark 1:17).

The Great Commission

Matthew 28:18-20 is called the Great Commission: "And Jesus came and spoke to them, saying, 'All authority has been given to Me in heaven and on earth. Go therefore and make disciples of all the nations, baptizing them in the name of the Father and of the Son and of the Holy Spirit, teaching them to observe all things that I have commanded you; and lo, I am with you always, even to the end of the age.' Amen."

Jesus mentioned two great commandments (to love God and to love your neighbor as yourself) and one Commission (to make disciples). Jesus was moved with compassion for hurting people: "But when He saw the multitudes, He was moved with compassion for them, because they were weary and scattered, like sheep having no shepherd," (Matthew 9:36), "And when Jesus went out He saw a great multitude; and He was moved with compassion for them, and healed their sick," (Matthew 14:14). The Apostle Paul explains to us in Romans how sin causes pain in people's lives: "For the wages of sin is death, but the gift of God is eternal life in Christ Jesus our Lord," (Romans 6:23). In the hearts of all believers there should be a desire for others to know Jesus Christ, the Savior of the world. Making disciples is a great privilege and an awesome responsibility.

Consider the following three verses.

"And anyone not found written in the Book of Life was cast into the lake of fire," (Revelation 20:15).

"Those who are wise shall shine like the brightness of the

firmament, and those who turn many to righteousness like the stars forever and ever," (Daniel 12:3).

"Then the master said to the servant, 'Go out into the highways and hedges, and compel them to come in, that my house may be filled,'" (Luke 14:23).

When we lead someone to Christ, eternity changes for them, for us, and for God!

- Instead of judgment, that person is forgiven and will go to heaven.
- We will have another brother or sister in heaven with us, and we will receive eternal commendation and reward (we will shine like the stars).
- God will be glorified in heaven by another son or daughter in His heavenly family.

This is truly an awesome responsibility! Jesus, the Light of the world (John 8:12), called us the light of the world (Matthew 5:14-16). It is God's will for us to spread the good news and for all people to believe (John 4:34-35). Even if people reject the gospel, preaching the gospel is still inherently good (Mark 16:15). However, the goal should always be to win souls to Jesus Christ.

What is Witnessing?

Ultimately, witnessing is simply sharing our faith. It is telling someone else the gospel, the good news that they can believe in Jesus Christ and be saved. The message that Jesus preached was simple: "Repent, for the kingdom of heaven is at hand," (Matthew 4:17). To paraphrase that, "God is a King in heaven, and His reign and authority have come near to your life. He cares enough about you to want to be your King. Turn from your sins, receive Him as your Sovereign, and believe in His Son. If you do, He will accept you into His kingdom, pardon you, and give you a new life. If you do not, there will be eternal damnation." (Part of the good news is the "bad news" about the reality of hell, eternal damnation, and the lake of fire.)

When Jesus Christ is honored as Lord, His authority is recognized; He is the boss. Being a disciple begins with a decision to follow Christ, but it does not stop there. A disciple is a learner, someone who is following Jesus and is learning from Him. We want others to share this joy. Preaching the gospel might look different for different people or circumstances. For example, it may involve telling others our testimony (in other words, how we met Jesus Christ). It may mean sharing Bible verses to answer questions or to meet a particular need. Or, it may be accompanied by listening, helping, showing concern, or praying for a sick person or for some other need. If you are one of those people who feels inadequate to witness, or not a good enough Christian or does not know the Bible well enough, take heart! The Bible makes it clear that we have something perfect (Jesus Christ) within an imperfect container (us). "But we have this treasure in earthen vessels, that the excellence of the power may be of God and not of us," (2 Corinthians 4:7). Everyone is inadequate or insufficient to witness, but God makes us adequate. "Not that we are sufficient of ourselves to think of anything as being from ourselves, but our sufficiency is from God, who also made us sufficient as ministers of the new covenant, not of the letter but of the Spirit; for the letter kills, but the Spirit gives life," (2 Corinthians 3:5-6). Clearly, God can use anyone!

The Bible often compares the sharing of our faith to planting and harvesting; see for example Psalm 126:5, Matthew 13:3-23, Mark 4:3-20, Luke 8:4-15, Matthew 13:24-30, 31-32, 37-43, and John 4:35-38. As with sowing seed, we should sow bountifully to reap bountifully (2 Corinthians 9:6). However, it is important to remember that we bring the good news of Jesus Christ, not human rules. Our Commission is to make people followers of Jesus. It is not to make everyone live more righteously, nor is it to convict people of their sin. Those tasks are the responsibility of Jesus Christ and the Holy Spirit. What we can do and what we are to do is proclaim and uphold God's righteous standard, His holiness, and His judgment, so that people can respond to the conviction of the Holy Spirit.

How Do We Witness?

You witness by sharing **your** faith, not that of someone else (Acts 19:13-16). All Christians have a testimony—that is, how they met Jesus Christ. You can share that—and you should share that, but share your faith, not your philosophy, not what you just read in a book, not your hobbies, opinions, etc. Our faith is what makes us excited about Jesus, so share your excitement about our thrilling, wonderful Lord Jesus Christ. Jesus said, "And I, if I am lifted up from the earth, will draw all peoples to Myself," (John 12:32). Like the saying that you have to catch a fish before you can clean it, people first must come, with their sins, to Jesus as their Savior. Only when Jesus saves us will He forgive us and set us free from our sins. If we demand that people become holy before they respond to Christ, we are asking for what the Bible says is impossible. Witnessing may bring to light what is keeping someone from Christ, but it is not supposed to point out every character flaw in a person's life. Instead, our witness should share our own faith and experience in the redemptive work of Christ with the burdened and hurting.

When Sharing Your Faith:

Be friendly—be friends with people without loving the world. We are to be separate from the world and its sin, but still have contact with unbelievers (1 Corinthians 5:9-11, John 17:15). The Christian life might be easier if we broke off all contact with unbelievers, but Jesus has called us to be His witnesses to and in the world.

Be kind—it is easier to catch flies with honey than with vinegar. Our words are to be gracious, but still mixed with the sobering truth of God's judgment (Colossians 4:5-6).

Be clear—tell people exactly what they must do to be saved (Acts 16:30). Do not tell people something vague, like "read the Bible and be a Christian and you'll get to heaven." Believing in Jesus is not vague. It is specific. People can confess with their mouths the Lord Jesus Christ and believe in their hearts that God raised Him from the dead (Romans 10:8-9). Jesus told the Laodiceans to open the door and He would come in (Revelation 3:20). People can open their lives to the rule (authority) of Christ. So speak clearly, and do not use religious terminology. Most people do not understand words like sanctification, propitiation, or high priest. "Christianese" can be confusing!

Be sure—know Whom you believe. Do not be afraid to insist that Jesus is the only way for people to get into heaven. He Himself said so: "Jesus said to him, 'I am the way, the truth, and the life. No one comes to the Father except through Me,'" (John 14:6). In such a statement, Jesus was either telling the truth or lying. If it was the truth, then any other religious figure is not the way (Acts 4:12). There is no need to discuss, criticize, or even mention the teachings, attributes, or shortcomings of anyone else. Only Jesus Christ, the Lamb of God, was found worthy to take the Book of Life and to open its seals (Revelation 5:2-9). Also, there are no second or third "go-rounds" to get it right or to achieve some level of spiritual enlightenment. In this life is the only opportunity to be saved; there is no such thing as reincarnation (Hebrews 9:27)!

Be simple—know and proclaim Jesus Christ and Him crucified (1 Corinthians 2:2). Do not get bogged down with discussions of doctrines (Matthew 7:6), and try to avoid being distracted from the subject of faith in Jesus Christ. Many people will want to talk about the Inuit or other isolated tribe, abstract philosophies, or evolution. However, the central question is not what the Inuit think about Jesus. Jesus said, "Who do you say that I am?" (Matthew 16:15). That is the real issue to focus on for each person: Is Jesus Christ your Lord?

Be excited—about Jesus! Even if you do not know many Bible verses, people will want the joy that you have.

Be bold—you are bringing words of eternal life. People will realize that you have had a supernatural experience with the Lord (Acts 4:13). Remember, boldness comes from being filled with the Holy Spirit (Acts 2:14; 6:5; 7:55).

Be willing to serve (Matthew 5:16). There is one church whose members deliberately ride elevators in large apartment buildings. They offer to help carry groceries as they do so, which allows an opportunity for them to then share the good news of Jesus Christ. As a result, the people they reach can see and hear the gospel in action.

Love people—have genuine concern for them. Jesus' love for people moved Him to action (Matthew 9:35-38)..

Stir up the gifts of the Holy Spirit. When you meet someone, look to God to bring His kingdom into their lives. Offer to pray for people if they have a need. When people are healed, delivered, or set free by a miracle or word of knowledge, they will be more open to salvation (John 4:17-18). Of course, that depends on God doing miracles! The Holy Spirit has given gifts to God's people according to His own will (Hebrews 2:4). Stepping out in faith to pray for people is a wonderful opportunity to see the gifts of the Holy Spirit functioning in our lives and ministering to those around us. People have said, "If you want to have the gifts of the Holy Spirit, get into situations where you need them." Witnessing is a great way to do that!

Minister faith—especially if people say they do not believe. Do not give a long teaching of what faith is. Minister faith: "You can be saved! You can believe!"

Be alert—God brings people into our lives. Such meetings with people have been called "divine appointments." Look for opportunities to share the gospel.

Pray for opportunities—to witness, to share your faith.

Pray for souls to be saved through your ministry. Solomon tells us that if we are wise we will win souls (Proverbs 11:30). God promises to give us wisdom if we ask Him in faith (James 1:5). Psalm 126:5-6 describes someone reaping a harvest after sowing seed with tears. If you are going into a situation where you will have an opportunity to share your faith, pray that people will receive the gospel.

Be abundant—let everyone know the good news (Ecclesiastes 11:1-2,6)! Some people have set goals of telling at least one person about Jesus every day or every week. Sometimes the message will be rejected, and sometimes it will be accepted. Jesus mentioned this process of sowing and reaping (John 4:37).

The Discipline of Compassion

Win souls, not arguments. Do not try to have all the answers, and avoid being drawn into contention. It is better to lose an argument and win a soul! If people feel that they have lost an argument, they may become defensive and closed to Jesus Christ. Instead, focus on sharing your own faith and personal experience with the Lord Jesus Christ.

Practice sharing your testimony aalone or in front of a mirror, if you are embarrassed to talk to someone.

Be creative—look for ways to share your faith. This applies to personal and public witnessing. Perhaps you and your friends can do a skit or pantomime in a school or other public place, using Biblical passages like the parables of Jesus or the account of Jesus raising Lazarus from the dead. A group of Christians can sing songs of praise and victory as they walk through town, like a parade. These praise marches can lead to many conversations about spiritual things. You could even have one or more public evangelistic meetings, with prayer for the sick, handing out Bibles, New Testaments, or tracts (booklets that give a gospel message). These events can be organized or unplanned. Consider making your own testimony tract. These are short (a few pages) accounts of how you came to believe in Christ.

Make leading statements—that bring Christ into the conversation. Create opportunities to witness by casually mentioning spiritual things during conversations. For example, in a conversation about today's weather, you could say something like, "I just love it when God gives us weather like this!" Another example might be, "I felt overwhelmed with all the material, so I asked the Lord to help me focus on what would be on the test. I didn't get to sleep until two in the morning!" If the other person is interested in spiritual things, he or she can respond to your comment about the Lord.

Use your secret weapons! We have been given some very powerful tools:

- Love never fails (1 Corinthians 13:8)!
- We can overcome the devil by the word of our testimony (Revelation 12:11).

Identify with people. "Weep with those who weep" (Romans 12:15). Use common interests or experiences to start a conversation and illustrate gospel truths. For example, "I used to drive a truck, too. It was not always easy to control a large vehicle. I realized that life can be the same way. We need someone who is always in control of our lives and the future. When I realized that only Jesus Christ can do that, I accepted Him as my heavenly Driver."

Meet people where they are.

- If someone is a Hindu or has believed Eastern philosophy, concentrate on the message of the cross (1 Corinthians 1:18-23). Jesus Christ suffered and died for our sins. Help them to see that there is no reincarnation (Hebrews 9:27), but only new life in Christ.

- If someone is a Catholic who has not been born again, point out that there is only one mediator, the Man Christ Jesus. "For there is one God and one Mediator between God and men, the Man Christ Jesus," (1 Timothy 2:5).

- If someone is self-righteous, tell them that all have sinned (Romans 3:23), and Jesus came to save sinners (Matthew 9:13).

- If someone thinks they can earn salvation, tell them that no flesh will be justified by works (Galatians 2:16).

- If someone thinks they are saved, but it is apparent that they are not, show them Scriptures that will reveal how they must be born again (John 3:3).

- If they are vehemently opposed to Christ, tell them that Jesus actually prefers cold people to lukewarm ones! He states that "I know your works, that you are neither cold nor hot. I could wish you were cold or hot," (Revelation 3:15). Then, challenge them to be honest and meet Jesus.

- If someone is angry at the evil in the world, remind them of our own choices and evil nature (Ecclesiastes 7:20-22, Romans 3:23). God has had mercy on us.

- If people are hurting or discouraged, offer them hope. We serve the God of hope (Romans 15:13).

- If people come from a culture where fear and power are the spiritual focus (for example, like in many countries in Africa), point out that Jesus Christ has all authority in heaven and on earth, including over every demon and the Devil himself! "And Jesus came and spoke to them, saying, 'All authority has been given to Me in heaven and on earth,'" (Matthew 28:18). Jesus is the King of kings and Lord of lords (1 Timothy 6:15, Revelation 17:14; 19:16). At the name of Jesus every knee shall bow (Philippians 2:10-11). Jesus has authority over every spirit, curse, or evil force. When people turn to Jesus, they can live a life of joy and liberty, free from fear of evil spirits.

- If people come from a culture where shame and honor are of great importance, explain that God has seen all our shameful and dishonorable behavior; we cannot hide from Him. But there is good news! Jesus suffered shame on the cross so He could take away our shame (Hebrews 12:2). He alone offers us honor in place of shame: "Instead of your shame you shall have double honor, and instead of confusion they shall rejoice in their portion. Therefore in their land they shall possess double; Everlasting joy shall be theirs," (Isaiah 61:7).

Finally, some people may try to put the responsibility for their problems on you, or to use your weaknesses as an excuse not to follow Christ. If someone does these things, just continue to point them to Jesus (2 Corinthians 4:5).

Scriptures to Use When Sharing Your Faith

John 3:3—we must be born again.

John 3:16—God so loved the world that He gave His Son.

Acts 4:12—there is no other name by which we are saved.

Romans 3:23—all have sinned.

Romans 6:23—the wages of sin is death, eternal life is a gift.

Romans 10:8,9—believe and confess to be saved.

Ephesians 2:8,9—we are saved by grace through faith, not works.

Revelation 3:20—ask Jesus into your heart. (This Scripture can be used as a starting point in a person turning to the Lord. Repentance and surrender to Christ must accompany this invitation.)

It is good to become familiar with verses that are meaningful to you, so that you can then share the verse itself with whomever you are witnessing. When you are using Scriptures, it is generally best not to quote the references. They are usually meaningless to unbelievers, unless, in addition, you are actually showing them the verses in the Bible.

To Whom Do We Witness?

The best people to reach out to are the people around us—who will generally be our family, friends, and co-workers. We can understand their needs better than anyone else. As a result, God has picked special Christians to send to them: us! Most people attend church because they were invited by a friend, not because they attended an evangelistic meeting. This is not to devalue evangelistic meetings. They are scriptural, effective, and necessary. However, do not restrict sharing your faith to evangelistic meetings! People are open to the gospel when going through trials, such as career changes, job loss, death of a loved one, severe illness, financial problems, legal difficulties, or relocation. Be sensitive to opportunities for the gospel in those situations! Whether those people receive Christ or not, we still need to show them the love of God, so be available to do your part to help them (Matthew 25:31-46). Although these people can be the most receptive, everyone needs to hear the gospel. So remember to share with everyone! Even if that in situations of severe persecution, share, asking God for boldness (Acts 4:29) and to be led by the Holy Spirit.

In Summary

Have compassion for people—their present hurts and their future eternal destruction—and share the good news of the Savior, Jesus Christ. Be excited about Jesus, be understanding of people's needs, be alert for opportunities to witness, and let your light shine brightly!

6. Giving
The Discipline of Dependence

Giving is a characteristic of God Himself (John 3:16). In the Scriptures (Psalms 112:9 and 2 Corinthians 9:9), it is listed in connection with Christ's eternal righteousness. Giving (when we are not trying to get something back in return) requires that we have an eternal, heavenly perspective. This is because, as we give, we are committing our things to the Lord, which takes faith and trust in Him (Proverbs 19:7). Jesus told the rich young ruler, "If you want to be perfect, go, sell what you have and give to the poor, and you will have treasure in heaven; and come, follow Me," (Matthew 19:21). When our lives are over, we will ultimately leave all earthly treasures behind. However, as we give in our earthly life, we are storing up future treasure in heaven (Matthew 6:19,20).

The Bible teaches us sharing (Hebrews 13:16), generosity (2 Corinthians 9:5), and that we will reap what we sow: "He who sows sparingly will also reap sparingly, and he who sows bountifully will also reap bountifully," (2 Corinthians 9:6). Jesus Himself tells us that "It is more blessed to give than to receive," (Acts 20:35), and to "Give, and it will be given to you: good measure, pressed down, shaken together, and running over will be put into your bosom. For with the same measure that you use, it will be measured back to you," (Luke 6:38).

When considered closely, Biblical giving falls into three categories: tithes, offerings, and almsgiving. Tithing is giving one tenth, usually ten percent of our income; offerings are contributions (to the Lord, to His work, or to His workers) beyond that ten percent; and almsgiving is giving to the poor. However, giving to the rich (giving in the hope of receiving some kind of repayment), is not Scriptural (Proverbs 22:16).

Tithing

Tithing (literally, "giving a tenth") is first recorded in the Bible when Abraham gave a tenth to Melchizedek (Genesis 14:20). The Lord, through Moses, eventually made tithing a law for the Israelites (Leviticus 27:30), which enabled the Levitical priesthood to live and perform their service to the Lord. Interestingly, although testing the Lord is forbidden, in the matter of tithing He actually invited the Hebrews to test Him, to see if He would reward them for tithing.

> *"Will a man rob God? Yet you are robbing Me! But you say, 'How have we robbed You?' In tithes and offerings. You are cursed with a curse, for you are robbing Me, the whole nation of you! Bring the whole tithe into the storehouse, so that there may be food in My house, and test Me now in this," says the LORD of hosts, "if I will not open for you the windows of heaven and pour out for you a blessing until it overflows. Then I will rebuke the devourer for you, so that it will not destroy the fruits of the ground; nor will your vine in the field cast its grapes," says the LORD of hosts. All the nations will call you blessed, for you shall be a delightful land," says the LORD of hosts.*
> Malachi 3:8-12 (NAS)

That is indeed a wonderful promise! On the other hand, what is the consequence of withholding our tithe? Malachi 3 actually calls failure to tithe "robbing God," and cites it as a reason for financial problems!

In the New Testament, tithing is not commanded—but giving is. It may be that Jesus assumed that tithing was understood to be a requirement: "Woe to you, scribes and Pharisees, hypocrites! For you pay tithe of mint and anise and cummin, and have neglected the weightier matters of the law: justice and mercy and faith. These you ought to have done, without leaving the others undone," (Matthew 23:23). However, giving to those in ministry is clearly commanded (1 Corinthians 9:14, Matthew 10:10, Luke 10:7, 1 Timothy 5:18). The principle does not change from that of tithing; indeed, it is an intricately linked facet. The work of the Lord and His workers requires money, which God provides for His people. God's people have the responsibility and opportunity to give to the Lord, and thus bless the work of the Lord and store up eternal riches (1 Timothy 6:18,19). Many believe that, by tithing, they will receive the blessings promised in Malachi 3. If you share that conviction, then tithe! However, if you are tithing because you feel under compulsion, or someone is making you feel guilty, then reconsider. God loves a cheerful giver (2 Corinthians 9:7), and His blessing is on what is done by faith, not by guilt (Romans 14:23). Although tithing is good when it is done in faith, keep in mind that Jesus' standards were much higher than those of Moses. For example, whereas Moses commanded not to commit adultery, Jesus taught that looking at a woman lustfully is already committing adultery in one's heart; Moses taught to love your neighbor and hate your enemies; Jesus taught to love your enemies. Jesus commended the poor widow who put in her last coins into the temple treasury (Mark 12:41-44).

Scripture also discusses the principle of the "first fruits." The first ripe fruits of the Jewish harvest belonged to the Lord (Exodus 23:19), and this included the first born: "Consecrate to Me all the firstborn, whatever opens the womb among the children of Israel, both of man and beast; it is Mine," (Exodus 13:2). Giving the first fruits back to God is an acknowledgment of Him as the Source of our blessings. Simultaneously, it is a dependence on Him for the future. Thus, the tithe belongs to God (Leviticus 22:30-32). We must understand that, as believers, whatever money we possess really belongs to God (Haggai 2:8). Then, giving becomes much easier!

Offerings

Offerings are given to the Lord out of a free will, not as a tithe (Genesis 8:20). In the Law of Moses, some offerings were payments for sin, while others were expressions of gratefulness (Exodus 20:24; 29:14). In the New Testament, sacrificial living and giving one's life for Christ are mentioned as offerings (Romans 15:16, Ephesians 5:2, Philippians 2:17), as are thanksgiving and praise (Hebrews 13:15). In addition, several instances of giving to the church leadership are also noted as types of offerings (Acts 2:44-45; 4:34-37). All these seem to be far beyond giving ten percent. For example, before being scattered by persecution (Acts 8), a number of the saints gave away their possessions (Acts 4:34-37). These possessions would have ultimately been left behind when the believers were forced out of Jerusalem, and, thus, the saints had the opportunity to turn something very temporary—their earthly possessions—into eternal reward!

Almsgiving

In Matthew 6:2-3, Jesus gives us the instruction to give to the poor. Furthermore, He said to "give alms of such things as you have," (Luke 11:41), and even to "sell what you have and give alms," (Luke 12:33). It is likely that He Himself had a habit of giving to the poor (John 13:29), and that the believers in the New Testament followed His example in their own contributions to the poor and needy (Acts 11:29-30, Romans 15:26, 1 Corinthians 16:3, 2 Corinthians 8:4, 19-20). The Apostle Paul desired to help the poor, which other leaders encouraged him to do (Galatians 2:10); he devoted considerable attention during his ministry to making a collection to help the poor saints (2 Corinthians 8 and 9).

Incidentally, many beggars are quite familiar with Jesus' words about giving. Do not let such people manipulate you into giving when you are not inclined to do so. We give because the Lord commands giving and because He puts His concern in our hearts for the poor—not because someone is trying to make us feel guilty! If you are inclined to give, then give—even to such people—and be free not to give (for example, if you know they will spend it only on alcohol). Our church used to meet in a section of a city with many panhandlers. After watching some of them get drunk on alcoholic beverages they had purchased with our money, we restricted our giving to giving what they needed: If they said they needed food, we purchased food and gave it to them; if they needed a bus ticket, we purchased a non-refundable bus ticket and gave it to them as they boarded the bus.

Chapter 6: Giving

How to Give

How should a believer give? A good start is to give ten percent of all your income to the Lord, which usually means offering a tithe to the local church. There are certain situations where this is not possible or advisable, so that in these cases it is appropriate for the tithe to go instead to a specific work or ministry with which you are familiar. Beyond tithing, be ready to also make contributions to ministries or projects to advance the kingdom of God (Titus 3:1). Proverbs 3:27 tells us "Do not withhold good from those to whom it is due, when it is in the power of your hand to do so." Instead, have a desire to help the poor!

It is important to keep in mind that, as a believer, you are responsible for being a good steward of the Lord's money. You should give to what you believe is the Lord's work (whether that be world evangelization or feeding the poor, for example), and you should take care that the money you give is being handled properly (honestly and responsibly). It is reasonable to want a general accounting for what you give (or for what money a ministry receives), but the ultimate responsibility for what is done with contributions lies with the one receiving the contributions. Indeed, consider how Jesus still let Judas Iscariot carry the money bag for the disciples, even though Judas was pilfering from it (John 12:6). Do not let concern about responsible financial management keep you from giving! Ultimately, we give because Jesus commanded us to give.

> *"Give to him who asks of you, and do not turn away from him who wants to borrow from you."*
>
> Matthew 5:42 42

Jesus did not take time to described the qualifications of those worthy or not of receiving our money! However, if do you find that you are concerned about the use of your contributions, one of the best ways to be sure the Lord's money entrusted to you is being used wisely is to give only to ministries you are personally familiar with. If you know someone to be faithful, then you can give with assurance.

Moreover they did not require an account from the men into whose hand they delivered the money to be paid to workmen, for they dealt faithfully."

2 Kings 12:15

Summary

Giving is commanded by the Lord, whether that takes the form of tithes, offerings, or almsgiving. To give to someone with no expectation of repayment from them requires faith. Ultimately, all the resources we have are the Lord's; understanding that makes it much easier to give what we have to others! God knows our heart, He sees what we are doing, and He will reward us for our generosity.

7. Fellowship
The Discipline of Friendship and Unity

God Himself, although one God and one Being, exists as three Persons. These three Persons have always existed in community with each other. The heavenly host (including angels, cherubim, seraphim, and whatever other beings are among them) also exist in community – both with the Three and with one another. We know from the Scriptures that when man was created, it was not good for him to be alone (Genesis 2:18). It is not only God's will; it is God's way and His very nature to dwell in community. Likewise, we are to be in relationship with other believers.

Membership in the Body of Christ

Fellowshipping with other members of the Church (or the Body of Christ, referring to all believers in Jesus Christ) is a great privilege. The Apostle Paul tells us that "…He put all things under His feet, and gave Him to be head over all things to the church, which is His body, the fullness of Him who fills all in all," (Ephesians 1:22-23). As Christians, we are given grace to function properly in that body (Romans 12:3-6, Ephesians 4:4-7). While the "body of Christ" consists of all the believers in the world, the local church is the expression of part of that body. Each of us must be involved with the local church if we are to relate properly with the heavenly Head of the body (Ephesians 4:15-16). Since each of us is different, we all have a specific part to play in the body (1 Corinthians 12:16-20, 27), and our participation or absence can have an effect on the entire body (1 Corinthians 12:26). The local church is given to us as a field of ministry, a protection, and a place of teaching, comfort, prayer, and restoration. Relating to other Christians helps us all to do good works and to conquer sin as a community in Christ (Hebrews 3:13; 10:24-25).

Fellowship with other believers is not limited to attending church on Sunday mornings, but includes informal times of being together, small group meetings, praying together (in person, over the phone, or online), and discussing the Bible with friends. If you choose to join in large group meetings, they are often very uplifting and can be wonderful times of celebration, while small groups can afford more personal interaction and intimacy. Both types of fellowship are important and scriptural (Acts 2:46).

The Bible warns us against ceasing to fellowship and meet together as Christians (Hebrews 10:25). Sin is deceitful—it can harden our hearts (Hebrews 3:13) and it can make us bitter (Hebrews 12:15). We can help each other to maintain a heavenly, eternal focus (Romans 15:14); indeed, we are instructed to restore one another (Galatians 6:1). "Confess your trespasses to one another," the book of James tells us, "and pray for one another, that you may be healed. The effective, fervent prayer of a righteous man avails much," (James 5:16). By following the Scripture's instruction, we can help each other to be overcomers in Christ.

We know we are forgiven when we confess our sins to God. When, in addition, other Christians pronounce us forgiven, we often experience a special feeling of cleansing and grace. (John 20:23). Exposing spiritual darkness through confession is often the most important step to achieving spiritual victory (John 1:5; 3:19-21, Ephesians 5:11-14), and the relationships and confidentiality of small group settings can enable us to confess our sins and struggles with one another. In these times of close fellowship, Christians can pray for us, and we for them, as we share our needs or the needs around the world. Small group Bible studies can give everyone an opportunity to participate—to share and to ask questions.

Ultimately, being with other believers helps to develop the character of Christ within us. Jesus commanded us to love one another (John 13:34), and each of us must learn to humble himself (or herself), to serve, to listen, and to love and care for one another (Romans 12:10, 1 Peter 5:5). As we do this, we grow in Christ and are better able to help others. We learn to counsel, and we develop habits of caring and sharing. These are all aspects of God's character.

The phrase "going to church" can be misleading. According to the Bible, we (believers in Christ) are the church—a building is not the church. As such, do not be afraid to meet with other believers without a pastor, elder, deacon, or other "official" present (assuming that your fellowship is not intended to create strife within the church or church leadership). If you are a believer in Jesus Christ, the Lord is with you. In the New Testament, believers met from house to house for informal Bible studies, fellowship, and food (Acts 2:42-46). We can—and should—still follow their example today: "Brethren, join in following my example, and note those who so walk, as you have us for a pattern," (Philippians 3:17).

However, when we meet together, some guidelines are still useful. For example, men and women should not meet together alone, so as to avoid temptation and the appearance of evil (1 Thessalonians 5:22, 2 Timothy 2:22). Meetings should start on time to honor the members of the body of Christ, and the place of preeminence should always be given to Jesus Christ (Colossians 1:18). The Bible sets no limits on how long or short a meeting should be . Indeed, Paul shared all night at least once (Acts 20:7-11). Therefore, we should have grace for those who want to have long meetings or to tarry at a particular meeting because of zeal, hunger, desperation, or because they are experiencing an encounter with God—and we should have grace for those who have to leave.

One basic rule sums up being with other believers: Do it! Withdrawing from fellowship results from selfishness or feeling rejected or hurt, and from putting our desires before the will of God (Proverbs 18:1). Do not allow yourself to make up excuses! Although it is often tempting to work every day to "get ahead," we need to take the time to meet with other believers at least once a week. Otherwise, our focus can shift to worldly things (like materialism, sexual immorality, and ambition), instead of heavenly things. Missing a meeting should be the exception in our lives, not the rule. Do not skip church without clear leading of the Holy Spirit. If you find yourself hesitant to attend a meeting, still go! You will meet with other believers and the Lord Himself, and you will be blessed (Matthew 18:20). However, if you are indeed certain the Holy Spirit is telling you not to go, then ask Him how else you can serve Him during that time.

Friendship

We need fellowship for both our character development and our mental health! This takes time and energy. As believers, we have the opportunity to develop deep, lasting relationships because of the spiritual unity we share in Christ. Many societies do not afford opportunities for healthy relationships to develop. Therefore, it is important that we make the effort to reach out to others and cultivate friendships. Times of ministry, informal talks, and recreational activities are important ways of building relationships. These are not to replace, but are to supplement, times with our families. Men can support, encourage, and exhort one another through healthy, wholesome friendships; likewise, women can help each other. It is good for people to have close relationships with others of the same sex; if they do not, they can become easily discouraged, or even develop unhealthy relationships with those of the opposite sex. The writer of Proverbs tells us that "A man who has friends must himself be friendly, but there is a friend who sticks closer than a brother," (Proverbs 18:24). Thus, take time to be a friend! It may not be easy, but it will be rewarding.

Summary

The admonitions to fellowship and to cultivate relationships with other believers are for our own good and for the good of the body of Christ. Indeed, they are key components of the command to love each other. "A new commandment I give to you, that you love one another; as I have loved you, that you also love one another," (John 13:34). Resisting demonic pressure and our own tendencies (from weariness, shyness, or discouragement) to withdraw from others will keep us from being isolated and becoming an easy target for the enemy of our souls.

Conclusion

This book has set forth a framework for exercising diligence to make our call and election sure (2 Peter 1:10). The disciplines discussed are neither complicated nor difficult, and accepting the challenge to regularly do them will facilitate our spiritual growth and fruitfulness. As the apostle Paul exhorted Timothy, his true son in the faith (1 Timothy 1:2), "Meditate on these things; give yourself entirely to them, that your progress may be evident to all. Take heed to yourself and to the doctrine. Continue in them, for in doing this you will save both yourself and those who hear you," (1 Timothy 4:15-16).

May God give you all grace through Jesus Christ as you seek Him!

Made in the USA
Middletown, DE
01 December 2023

43867365R10040